SCIENTISTS AND THEIR DISCOVERIES

GREGOR MENDEL

SCIENTISTS AND THEIR DISCOVERIES

SCIENTISTS AND THEIR DISCOVERIES

GREGOR MENDEL

GEORGE WILMER

MASON CREST

Mason Crest
450 Parkway Drive, Suite D
Broomall, Pennsylvania 19008
(866) MCP-BOOK (toll-free)
www.masoncrest.com

CPSIA Compliance Information: Batch #SG2018.
For further information, contact Mason Crest at 1-866-MCP-Book.

First printing
9 8 7 6 5 4 3 2 1

Library of Congress Cataloging-in-Publication Data
ISBN: 978-1-4222-4030-4 (hc)
ISBN: 978-1-4222-7762-1 (ebook)

Scientists and their Discoveries series ISBN: 978-1-4222-4023-6

NATIONAL
HIGHLIGHTS

Developed and Produced by National Highlights Inc.
Interior and cover design: Yolanda Van Cooten
Production: Michelle Luke

QR CODES AND LINKS TO THIRD-PARTY CONTENT

CONTENTS

KEY ICONS TO LOOK FOR:

Words to understand: These words with their easy-to-understand definitions will increase the reader's understanding of the text while building vocabulary skills.

Sidebars: This boxed material within the main text allows readers to build knowledge, gain insights, explore possibilities, and broaden their perspectives by weaving together additional information to provide realistic and holistic perspectives.

Educational Videos: Readers can view videos by scanning our QR codes, providing them with additional educational content to supplement the text. Examples include news coverage, moments in history, speeches, iconic sports moments and much more!

Text-dependent questions: These questions send the reader back to the text for more careful attention to the evidence presented there.

Research projects: Readers are pointed toward areas of further inquiry connected to each chapter. Suggestions are provided for projects that encourage deeper research and analysis.

Series glossary of key terms: This back-of-the book glossary contains terminology used throughout this series. Words found here increase the reader's ability to read and comprehend higher-level books and articles in this field.

For thousands of years, humans have used a process called selective breeding to develop particular traits, or characteristics, in plants and animals. An Austrian friar named Gregor Mendel was the first to accurately describe the process of heredity: how characteristics are passed on from parent to offspring.

WORDS TO UNDERSTAND

genetics—the science of genes and heredity.

hybridization—to make hybrids by crossing unlike parents.

lime burner—a person who heated and processed limestone in order to make quicklime, a substance used to make mortar and plaster used for building.

variety—plants or animals that differ from other members of their species.

CHAPTER 1

Education of a Scientist

There is a 5,000-year-old Persian seal inscribed with horses' heads that shows a record of inheritance of mane and head shape through several generations. In England, Robert Bakewell (1725–95) founded a famous herd of longhorn cattle by inbreeding: mating animals that were similar in order to emphasize certain characteristics, such as size and color. In North America, Native Americans improved their maize crop by outbreeding—crossing two unlike **varieties** of corn to get a variety with the qualities of both.

Sometimes these methods of selective breeding for inherited characteristics were successful. But sometimes the offspring would be more like one parent than the other, sometimes the offspring would be a mixture, and, sometimes, the offspring would be a "throwback" to a grandparent. Thus, selective breeding worked in practice, but the reasons for its success or failure were not understood.

In 1865, a friar named Gregor Mendel explained in his writings how characteristics (in his writings, he called them "characters") were inherited, how heredity depended on sexual reproduction, and how the inheritance of likenesses followed simple mathematical rules. This is the basis of the modern science of **genetics**. By following Mendel's rules, it is possible to understand how the size of corncobs, the quality of a horse's mane, or the color patterns of a cow's coat are inherited.

The rules of genetics that Mendel pioneered have been found to apply to all plants and all animals. But inheritance in humans is not as easy to study as it is

A small cob of maize remains among shards of pottery at an ancient Native American dwelling site in Utah. At the time maize was initially domesticated by Native Americans in Mexico, about 10,000 years ago, ears of maize, containing the kernels, were only about an inch long. Today, thanks to millennia of selective breeding, the ears are roughly seven times that size.

in animals or plants. A scientist cannot arrange marriages to study why children with albinism are born in one family, deaf and non-verbal children in another family, and children with blond hair and blue eyes in another. The geneticist must get his information from the results of marriages that have happened. But mathematical techniques have been invented for analyzing this sort of information.

Mendel's biographer Hugo Iltis said that Mendel searched through the parish registers of Brno to find inherited characteristics in residents. There is no evidence that he found what he was looking for. But the mathematical rules of chance that Mendel proved to work in the inheritance of color, shape, and size of pea plants have been found to apply equally to humans.

Early Life

Among the rolling hills of what today is the Czech Republic is a small village called Hynčice. In the nineteenth century, this region was part of the Austrian Empire, and the village was called by the German name of Heinzendorf bei Odrau. The people who lived in the village were farmers and **lime burners**. One of the farmers was named Anton Mendel. His ancestors had been living in the village since 1684.

As a young man, Anton had been in the Austrian Army. When he came back to Hynčice, he took over a plot numbered 58 in the village and built a house with a tiled roof. He farmed about forty acres of sloping meadow: plowing the fields, cultivating crops, and trying to improve his stock of farm animals.

Anton was interested in growing fruit. He planted fruit trees in a field that sloped down from his house to the road. Anton experimented with grafting new varieties of fruit, exchanging grafts and stock as well as advice with the priest in nearby Vražné (then called Gross-Petersdorf).

In 1818, Anton married Rosine, the daughter of a gardener in the village. In July 1822, their son Johann was born. He was their second child and only son.

As a boy Johann attended the village school in Hynčice. The schoolmaster, recognizing that Johann was much cleverer than the other boys, persuaded Anton and Rosine to send him to a bigger school. So when Johann was eleven, he went to the Piarist College in Lipnik, an upper elementary school, about

FRUIT GROWING

At the village school in Hynčice, the principles of fruit growing were taught. It was unusual for a small village to have a school in those days. It was even more unusual to have one where the scientific principles of agriculture were taught.

The home in which Johann Mendel was born in Hynčice. At the time, this village was in the Austrian Empire; today, it is part of the Czech Republic.

twelve miles (twenty kilometers) from Hynčice. Again, Johann stood out from the other students. After a year in Lipnik, he was recommended for the Imperial Royal Gymnasium in Opava (then called Troppau), a high school about thirty-one miles (fifty kilometers) to the north of Hynčice.

Anton Mendel needed his son to work on the farm, but he agreed to let him be educated. Anton was not rich and could not afford the full fees for the high school, so Johann was entered on half rations. This meant he would have much smaller meals than the other students. But whenever the farmer came to Opava, he brought Johann a supply of fresh food from the farm. In this way, Johann managed to work through the first four "grammatical" classes at Opava.

Johann's school work was excellent. He was always graded first class with distinction and he qualified for the "humanities" classes of the upper school.

However, by this time Anton was unable to pay for his son's education at all. He had been injured by a rolling tree trunk and was never again able to work his farm profitably. From the age of sixteen, Johann had to fend for himself. He became a qualified private tutor and, by giving private lessons to other students while at the same time attending school himself, managed for a time. But the hard mental work and inadequate food made him ill, and in the spring of 1839, Johann went home to the farm to work in the fields. After a few months, he was able to return to Opava. He completed his studies and left the high school in 1840 with a certificate of excellence.

Johann, at eighteen, now wanted to study philosophy at the University Philosophical Institute of Olomouc (then called Olmütz). He intended to pay for this by earning money from private tutoring again. But "all his efforts remained unsuccessful," he wrote of himself later, "because of lack of friends and

A view of Lipnik, the village where eleven-year-old Johann attended the upper elementary school.

Johann Mendel attended religious services at this Roman Catholic church in Opava while he was attending the gymnasium, or high school, there.

recommendations." This disappointment made him ill again and this time, he spent a year at home on the farm to recover.

By 1841, Anton had to give up his farm. He sold it to Alois Sturm, the husband of his elder daughter Veronica. In turning over the farm, Anton also made provisions for Johann and for his younger daughter Theresia. Johann's share included a small sum of money if he "should enter the priesthood, or should in any other way begin to earn an independent livelihood." Theresia gave her share of the property to Johann. With this and the private tutoring work he eventually obtained, he was able to study philosophy at Olomouc.

"By a mighty effort," Johann wrote about himself, "he succeeded in completing two years of philosophy." But Johann was exhausted and "realized that it was impossible for him to endure such exertions any further." He could no longer put up with the insecurity of making his own way. "Therefore, after having finished his philosophical studies, he felt himself compelled to step into a station of life which would free him from the bitter struggle for existence." Johann followed the recommendation his father had made in 1841 and decided to enter the priesthood. "His circumstances decided his vocational choice," he wrote.

On July 14, 1843, the professor of physics at Olomouc University, Friedrich Franz, wrote to a colleague at Brno (then called Brünn), the capital city of Moravia. He was answering an inquiry about suitable candidates for the priesthood. He wrote that he could recommend only one. "This is Johann Mendel, born at Heinzendorf in Silesia. During the two year course in philosophy he has had, almost invariably, the most unexceptionable reports and is a young man of very solid character."

Olomouc was an important religious center in the Austrian Empire in the 1840s, when Mendel lived and studied at the university there. However, despite its ties to the German-speaking imperial and religious authorities, most residents of the city spoke the Czech language.

On October 9, 1843, Johann was admitted as a novice to the Augustinian monastery of Saint Thomas in Brno. He took a new name: Gregor.

The Monastery at Brno

The monastery at Brno was the intellectual center of Moravia. The people spoke Czech, but most of the friars were German-speakers. Mendel had little knowledge of Czech but was "willing," as Professor Franz wrote, "to devote himself to the mastery of the language during the years of theological study."

Most of the friars taught either at the University of Brno or at the high school. Visiting professors lodged at the monastery. The abbot of the monastery, Cyril Franz Napp (1782–1868), was professor of eastern languages at the university. Aurelius Thaler (1796–1843) spent many years at the monastery, while a botanist

The Augustinian monastery of Saint Thomas in Brno. Mendel was admitted as a friar to the Order of Saint Augustine in 1843. Members of the order took vows of poverty, chastity, and obedience.

The Augustinian order that Mendel joined was based on the teachings of Saint Augustine of Hippo (354–430 CE), a Christian theologian who lived in the Roman Empire during the fourth and fifth centuries.

at the Brno Philosophical Institute. He had made an important collection of the Moravian flora. He died in 1843, so Mendel just missed his chance to study with him. But Thaler's collection of living plants in the monastery's botanic garden and the dried plants in the monastery's herbarium were at Mendel's disposal.

Mendel described himself studying these plants and the monastery's collection of local geological specimens: "His special liking for this field of natural science deepened the more he had the opportunity to become familiar with it."

Meanwhile his formal studies continued. In his first year, he attended, "with much liking and devotion," classes on church history, archaeology, and Hebrew. The problems of existence seemed solved and he "regained his courage and strength."

He knows how to live well
who knows how to p.. well.
~ St. ...e

Scan here for a short video on the life of an Augustinian friar:

In his second year at the monastery (when he was studying Greek, the Scriptures and Church Law), Mendel took the vows of obedience, chastity, and poverty, in accordance with the rule of Saint Augustine. The following year, he was able to extend his studies toward his own interests. As well as studying the Church's teachings, Mendel went to courses in agriculture (apple and grape growing in particular) at the Philosophical Institute at Brno. Franz Diebl (1770–1859), who gave the lectures, was interested in the improvement of plants by **hybridization**.

In his fourth and final year of instruction, Mendel studied the practical aspects of being a priest, such as teaching the catechism and preaching. He also learned Arabic, Syriac, and Chaldaic (the languages of Arabia, ancient Syria, and ancient Babylon). He was now twenty-five years old.

The following year, 1847, having been ordained a sub-deacon, Mendel was made parish priest of the collegiate church. But Mendel had problems as a parish priest. He was too sensitive, too nervous. He suffered at school and became ill. As parish priest he felt his parishoners' pain keenly and found it unbearable to attend the dying. His problems were not made easier having to preach in Czech when his native language was German.

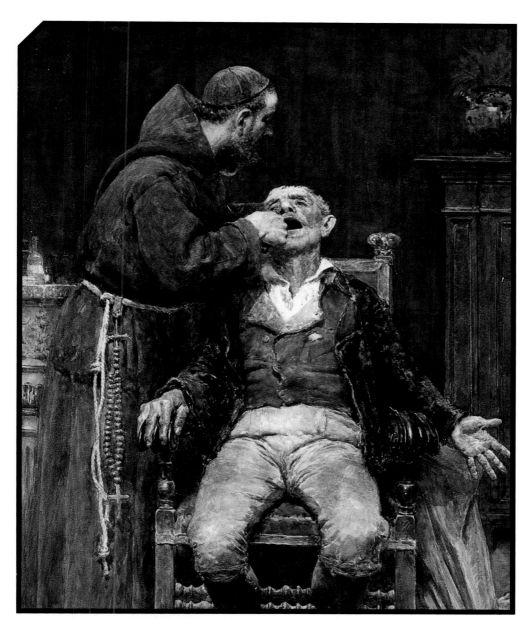

Unlike monks, who lived in self-sufficient communities and did not have regular contact with ordinary people, friars were expected to live and work within the larger community, teaching and engaging with the townsfolk. Here, a nineteenth-century friar removes a diseased tooth from a fellow citizen.

Mendel was sent as a substitute teacher to the high school in Znojmo. He could only be appointed to substitute positions until he passed the teachers' examination—a task he was never able to accomplish.

The abbot appreciated Mendel's intellectual abilities and sympathized with his problems as parish priest. He gave him permission to work for the degree of Doctor of Philosophy. The abbot then had Mendel appointed as a substitute teacher to the Imperial Royal High School in Znojmo (then called Znaim). German, not Czech, was the language of this wine-growing district near Vienna.

On October 9, 1849, Mendel took up his duties as substitute teacher. He taught Greek and elementary mathematics for twenty hours a week. Mendel's experience of private tutoring during his school days helped him to understand his pupils and he was a great success.

The schoolmaster appreciated his "vivid and lucid method of teaching" and offered to make him a permanent member of the staff. But he would have to pass the teachers' qualifying examination, which was usually taken after a course of training at a university. He had not had this training but, nevertheless, he was persuaded to try the examination in the summer of 1850. He asked to be examined in natural history and physics.

The examination was held by faculty of the University of Vienna and was in three parts. For the first part, candidates were given eight weeks to write two essays. This was a preliminary test. Only those candidates whose essays met the examiners' approval were invited to Vienna for the second and third parts of the examination. The two essay subjects that Mendel received were, for physics, on the chemical and physical properties of air and, for natural history, on volcanic and sedimentary rocks.

Mendel wrote and submitted his essays. The examiner in physics, Professor Baron von Baumgartner (1793–1865), reported that Mendel "writes simply, plainly and clearly, his method of exposition being orderly and lucid. If the other examiners are as well satisfied as I am, the candidate should have a very favorable testimonial."

But the professor of zoology, Rudolf Kner (1810–69), was not satisfied. Kner was influenced by the ideas of the great French paleontologist Georges Cuvier (1769–1832). The Frenchman regarded earth events as a series of independent creations, each brought to an end by some catastrophe of flood or fire or earthquake. In his view, there was no continuity. Kner was therefore unimpressed by Mendel's essay, in which he proposed, "the Creative energy of the earth remains active. So long as its fires still burn and its atmosphere still moves, the history of its creation is not finished."

Despire Kner's reservations, Mendel was called to Vienna for the second part of the examination. However, when he arrived in Vienna, he found that the examiners had changed their minds. They had written to him, telling him to wait a year. However, since Mendel was already there, they permitted him to continue. By then, of course, Mendel was quite nervous.

Mendel again satisfied Professor Baumgartner with an essay on magnetism. For Professor Kner, he was asked to write an essay on the classification of mammals. Kner had already published a work on this subject but, in his essay, Mendel ignored the work of his examiner. He may never have heard of it. Mendel answered Kner's question according to what he remembered from a standard German work on the subject. He remembered the outline but was poor on detail and showed no interest in the theoretical aspects of classification. Mendel's "orderly and lucid" approach was not evident in this essay.

Mendel was called to the oral examination, but failed.

However, Professor Baumgartner had been impressed by Mendel's work and advised the abbot to send Mendel to the university at Vienna, where he would be able to try the qualifying examination again.

TEXT-DEPENDENT QUESTIONS

1. Where was Johann Mendel born?
2. What monastery admitted Johann as a novice in 1843?
3. Where did Gregor Mendel serve as parish priest in 1847?

RESEARCH PROJECT

When Gregor Mendel became a friar, he joined the Order of Saint Augustine. This was one of four major Roman Catholic religious organizations, called "mendicant orders," that were dedicated to teaching and preaching the gospel. Members of these orders were called friars; they lived together and shared ownership of their property. Using the internet or your school library, find out more about one of the four major mendicant orders: Augustinian, Dominican, Franciscan, or Carmelite. Write a two-page report and share it with your class.

The University of Vienna, founded by Duke Rudolph IV in 1365, is the oldest university in the German-speaking world. Mendel attended courses there from 1851 to 1853.

WORDS TO UNDERSTAND

algae—a plant without roots, stems, or leaves that makes its own food by photosynthesis, and is usually aquatic.

cell—the unit of structure and function of plants and animals. Made up of a complex of membranes and usually containing a nucleus. The outside is clearly limited by a membrane or cell wall.

cell theory—the theory that all plants and animals are made up of cells.

fertilization—the fusion of male and female germ cells.

CHAPTER 2

Vienna University

For four terms, 1851–53, Mendel was a student in the philosophical faculty in Vienna. World-famous men were lecturing in the sciences in Vienna at this time and Mendel attended their courses in mathematics, physics, and biology.

For experimental physics, he went to the lectures of Christian Doppler (1803–53). In 1845, Doppler had shown how the pitch of a sound can seem to vary when it is moving in relation to the listener. This is called the "Doppler effect." For example, when a whistling train approaches very fast, a person standing near the tracks will perceive a change in the note of its whistle. Doppler had been at Vienna University since 1850 and, in 1851 when Mendel attended his lectures, he was forty-eight and an acknowledged master. Although Doppler was interested mainly in the properties of sound and light waves, he was also interested in theoretical mathematics and geometry and lectured on these subjects.

Andreas von Ettingshausen (1796–1878) lectured on mathematical physics. He worked on problems in wave mechanics and, like Doppler, was interested in applying mathematics to physics. He was also an experimentalist and lectured on the use of apparatus and the design of experiments.

Mendel, with his distinct ability in physics, was greatly influenced by the mathematical approach to physics of these two men and influenced, too, by the methods of physical experiment. He acted as demonstrator in physics for a time and became familiar with the experimental method: to test an idea by a planned experiment.

Mendel attended Kner's zoology course. He also attended lectures in paleontology, systematic botany, and plant physiology. The plant physiology lectures, given by Franz Unger (1800–70), made the most impression. Unger was a revolutionary in the biological sciences. He did not believe in the permanence of species, but believed that the plant world had "gradually developed itself step by step." For this statement in *Botanical Letters* (1852), Unger was attacked by the Church and threatened with dismissal from the university.

Unger was a supporter of the **cell theory**. In 1838, Matthias Schleiden (1804–81) was looking for some underlying principle that would unify biology. Schleiden found it in the cell. Schleiden realized that all higher plants and animals were made up of cells, which could be considered both as individuals and as united and dependent on one another in a whole plant or animal. These cells, making up whole plants and animals, he considered to be similar also to the single cells of the lower green plants, the **algae**. In 1842, Karl Wilhelm von Nägeli (1817–91) had worked with Schleiden in Jena and had shown that cells divide and make more cells to give growth from the tips of plant shoots.

Scan here for information about Vienna:

Unger referred to the work of both Schleiden and Nägeli in *Botanical Letters* and can, therefore, be presumed to have lectured on these subjects to his pupils in 1852.

In a later textbook, *Anatomy and Physiology of Plants* (1855), Unger described the processes of **fertilization**: the fusion of some element of maleness and some of femaleness. He wrote, too, about experiments in plant hybridization, the crossing of two unlike plants. He concluded that variations arose in natural populations and gave rise to new varieties and species.

So, during the four terms at Vienna University, Mendel learned that plants and animals are composed of

The Austrian botanist Franz Unger was professor of plant physiology at the University of Vienna from 1850 to 1852. His lectures had a strong influence on Mendel.

cells. He learned of experiments in plant hybridization. And he learned the methods of experimentation in physics. This was one of the most influential periods of his life.

Returning to the Monastery

In July 1853, Mendel returned to the monastery at Brno. He was soon appointed as substitute teacher to the new Technical Modern School in Brno. For the next fourteen years, he taught physics and natural history, always as a substitute teacher. He could never qualify in the teachers' examination at Vienna. In 1856, he tried again but became too nervous even to finish the written part of the examination. But he was a gifted teacher, loved and respected by his pupils, one of whom remembered years later the short fat friar with the twinkling gray eyes, dressed in a frock coat, trousers tucked into high boots and wearing a tall hat.

Before leaving Vienna, Mendel read a paper to the Zoological and Botanical Society on the moth *Botys margaritalis*, a pest of radishes. He had always been interested in crop improvement and the following year, 1854, he sent another paper on crop pests to the society. This was a short description of the pea weevil *Bruchus pisi*. Now he was elected a member of the Brno Agricultural Society and

DISCOVERING THE CELL

The discovery that living things are made up of tiny individual units was made by Robert Hooke around 1665. He was examining a very thin slice of cork through a microscope and saw that the cork was made up of a pattern of tiny rectangular holes. He described them as "much like a honeycomb…these pores or cells, were not deep but consisted of a great many little boxes." Hooke's "little boxes" were actually the outermost boundaries of the once-living plant cells and were all that remained after the cell had died. The word "cell" was kept to describe the entire living cell, however, and is one of the most important terms in biology.

Another of the investigators using the microscope was Antonie van Leeuwenhoek, a Dutch amateur scientist. Van Leeuwenhoek kept a draper's shop, but his favorite hobby was exploring the world of the very small with microscopes he made himself. He looked at just about everything from tooth scrapings to pond water. He was the first to could meet with local plant breeders and biologists from the university.

He started to make his own experiments in plant improvement on a small garden plot in the monastery. Soon he was crossing and selecting different varieties of peas and beans to improve their size and taste for the monastery table. By 1859, he had developed a variety of pea with bigger and sweeter seeds. The plants were fully fertile and easy to grow.

At meetings of the Natural Science Section of the Agricultural Society, discussions were often on topics of more theoretical interest. Members argued about the problems of fertilization and reproduction in plants and animals, about growth and development. Franz Unger became a member of the society in 1857.

discover the tiny organisms called "protozoa," in 1677. These were too small to be seen without the microscope. In 1683 van Leeuwenhoek made another great discovery. He described tiny structures that were at the absolute limit of the power of his microscope. From these descriptions we now know that what he saw were bacteria, the smallest of all living things. No one else would see bacteria for another 100 years.

In 1838, German botanist Matthias Schleiden made careful studies of plants under the microscope. He saw that all plants were composed of cells. The following year, 1839, Theodor Schwann, another German scientist, put forward the cell theory. In it he said that all living things are made up of cells or of material formed by cells and that each cell contains certain essential components. Because Schleiden had come up with more or less the same idea in connection with plants the previous year, both men are now given equal credit for the cell theory.

Matthias Jacob Schleiden is recognized as one of the founders of cell theory, along with a fellow German scientist, Theodor Schwann.

Under the influence of Unger's work, Mendel had become interested in the cultivation of wild plants. Unger believed that species could change and he wondered how they could change. One possibility was that change could be brought about by hybridization: two species could be combined to produce a new one. Another possibility was that change could be brought about by outside influences.

These outside influences could be, for plants, the nature of the soil in which they were growing, the amount of sunlight they received, the amount of rainfall. Some biologists, the most famous of whom was Jean-Baptiste de Lamarck (1744–1829), believed that these outside influences changed the form

Swiss botanist Karl Wilhelm von Nägeli taught at major universities in Zurich, Freiburg, and Munich. He and Mendel corresponded during the 1860s and 1870s, discussing Mendel's research into heredity, which Nägeli did not fully understand.

of the plant or animal and affected the whole organism so that its changed form would be permanent and passed on to its offspring. In this way, they thought, species could be changed into new species by the direct effect of outside conditions.

Unger did not believe this. He had found from his own experiments that, although some species grew bigger or smaller according to the conditions of cultivation, others kept their characteristics in spite of being grown under new conditions.

A garden in St Thomas's Abbey where Gregor Mendel grew peas for the monastery. He lived in a room on the first floor above the garden.

Mendel repeated these experiments of Unger, bringing varieties of wildflowers into the monastery garden to grow under controlled conditions. He grew specimens of two lesser *celandine* species next to one another, in exactly the same conditions, for several seasons and found that they kept their separate characteristics. He must, therefore, have agreed with Unger who had written in *Botanical Letters*, "The endeavor to trace the diversities of species to the effects of outward influences, such as the nature of the soils, assuredly misses the true cause."

Mendel is said to have told a colleague at school that "nature makes little progress in the formation of species in this way: hence it must be something somewhat different."

Having reached this decision, Mendel looked for the "something somewhat different" in the outcome of hybridization experiments.

TEXT-DEPENDENT QUESTIONS

1. What is the Doppler effect?
2. What did Franz Unger lecture on at the University of Vienna?
3. When did Mendel return to the monastery at Brno?

RESEARCH PROJECT

All living things are composed of cells. Take a virtual tour of a cell online at www.ibiblio.org/virtualcell/tour/cell/cell.htm.

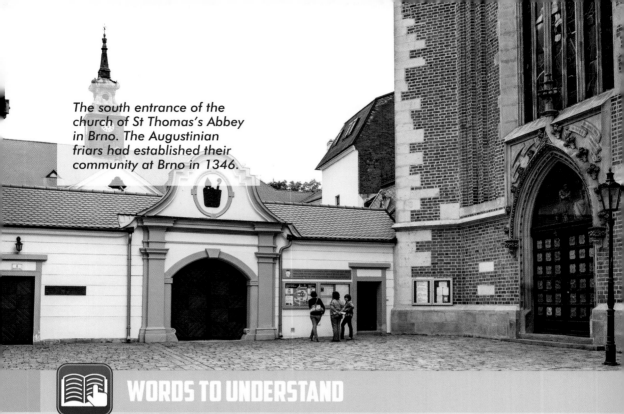

The south entrance of the church of St Thomas's Abbey in Brno. The Augustinian friars had established their community at Brno in 1346.

WORDS TO UNDERSTAND

back cross—a cross between an offspring and one of the parent types.

first filial generation, or F^1—the first generation of offspring from any cross.

first parental generation, or P^1—the individuals from which the first cross is made.

embryo—a developing plant or animal.

hybrid—the offspring of unlike parents.

nucleus—the part of the cell that contains the chromosomes.

second filial generation, or F^2—the generation produced by crossing individuals of the F^1 generation.

spermatozoon—the male germ cell. (Plural form, spermatoza.)

style—a long, slender stalk that rises from the ovary of a flowering plant. At the end of the style is the stigma, where pollen is deposited.

third filial generation, or F^3—the generation produced by crossing individuals of the F^2 generation.

CHAPTER 3

Important Influences on Mendel's Work

In the eighteenth century, most men believed that species of animals and plants were fixed. New species were not created under natural conditions—nor could they be created by man. But the results of hybridizing plants gave puzzling results.

Carl Linnaeus (1707–78), who for most of his life believed in the fixity of species, had seen two plant hybrids in the Botanic Gardens at Uppsala in Sweden. The unusual speedwell *Veronica* and the salsify-goat's beard plant *Tragopogon* were shown to be hybrids and to have some characteristics of both parents. Linnaeus believed these hybrids were new species and entered them in his *Species Plantarum* in 1753.

Experimental plant hybridization, however, started in 1760 when German biologist Joseph Gottlieb Kölreuter grew his first hybrids in Saint Petersburg, Russia.

In the introduction to his paper on plant hybridization, published in 1866, Mendel refers to the work of Kölreuter, as well as four other scientists.

Kölreuter's Studies

Kölreuter (1733–1806) knew that when two different plants were crossed, they could give rise to hybrids. He did not believe that these hybrids would breed more like themselves and they were not, therefore, new species.

In the eighteenth century, Carl Linnaeus developed a binomial system of
Latin names to classify species of living organisms. The first part of the name is the
genus, a larger group of related organisms. The second part of the name identifies
a species with distinctly different characteristics within the genus. For example, the
scientific name of the pea plants that Mendel studied is Pisum sativum. Pisum is a
genus that includes several other species, such as Pisum abyssinicum and Pisum
fulvum. Sativum refers to a specific type of plant that bears edible seed pods.

Kölreuter started his work with tobacco plants. He took pollen from specimens of *Nicotiana rustica*, which has short flowers and a short **style,** and put it on the styles of specimens of *Nicotiana paniculata,* which has long flowers and a long style. From these crosses Kölreuter got seeds which grew into **hybrid** plants that were intermediate in character between the two parents. The plants were intermediate in the flower, which was neither short nor long but medium in length. The flower was neither red nor white in color, but pink. Both the branching of the plant and the position of the flowers were intermediate between the parents.

Kölreuter measured and recorded thirteen characteristics, of which all except the form of the stamens were intermediate in the hybrid. But when Kölreuter's hybrid plants grew up, not one of them was self-fertile. The flower heads dropped off and there were no seeds. To Kölreuter, this was "one of the most wonderful of all events that have ever occurred upon the wide field of nature" because it seemed to prove that hybrids could not reproduce themselves.

But Kölreuter continued his experiments.

He examined the pollen of the hybrids and found it shrunken and obviously sterile. He could not tell by looking whether the ovaries were sterile or not. He

Scan here to learn more about botanist Carl Linnaeus:

German botanist Joseph Gottlieb Kölreuter was the first to demonstrate that pollen had to be transferred to the pistil of a plant for fertilization and reproduction to occur.

decided to test the fertility of the hybrid ovaries. He tried fertilizing hybrids with pollen from the parent species *Nicotiana rustica* and *Nicotiana paniculata* that were known to be fertile. The **first generation hybrid plant (F¹)** was crossed with one of the **parent plants (P¹)**. The **back cross**, in some cases, was successful. In such cases, Kölreuter had produced **second-generation hybrids (F²)**.

Second-generation hybrids can also result from the self-fertilization of hybrids of the first generation or from crosses between them. In the case of the tobacco plants, this type of cross could not be made because only the hybrid ovaries were fertile. But when Kölreuter crossed species of the flowering plant *Dianthus* (also called "pinks"), he got hybrid plants where both pollen and ovaries were fertile. F¹ hybrid *Dianthus* could be crossed to create F² hybrid *Dianthus*.

Kölreuter was the first man to make controlled crosses between species of plant and to follow these through two generations and to leave records of his experiments and of his results. His conclusions were that the first generation hybrids were like one another and intermediate between the two parents. He described the hybrid between a red-flower plant and a yellow-flower plant as "of mixed red and yellow. The flowers played into orange-yellow."

There was, however, one exception to intermediacy in Kölreuter's recorded experiments. In crosses between double-flower and single-flower *Dianthus* plants, the hybrids had double flowers. Kölreuter concluded that the pollen from the double flowers had the power of doubling the single ones.

This was the first recorded case in plants of a dominant characteristic. Double flowers were dominant to single flowers. But, as it was the only case Kölreuter found in his experiments, he merely observed and recorded it. For Kölreuter it was the intermediacy of all the other hybrids that was important.

Kölreuter had found that it did not matter which way around a cross was made: it did not matter which of the parents provided the pollen, which the ovary. He concluded, therefore, that male and female parents both contributed a share of "juices" to the offspring. Juices from the pollen and juices from the ovary combined to give an intermediate juice for the hybrid.

These pinkish "tobacco plant" flowers (Nicotiana tabacum) are similar to the hybrids produced by Kölreuter's crossbreeding experiments.

Illustration by William Herbert of a plant with flowering stems, Stenomesson humile, published in 1842.

In contrast to the similarity and uniformity of the first generation hybrids, Kölreuter found that second-generation hybrids F^2 were not all alike. Although they were created by self-fertilization of the F^1, they had different mixtures of characters and sometimes resembled one of the original parent plants P^1 more than the hybrid parent F^1. From this he concluded that hybrid juices of the F^1 combined in an irregular and unnatural way to produce the variety of the F^2 generation.

Kölreuter's experiments were, to him, evidence of the perfection of Nature. The intermediate F^1 hybrids showed the characters of one parent perfectly blended with those of the other. The breakdown of this perfection in the second generation was because man had interfered and was crossing plants "not intended for one another by the wise Creator."

Kölreuter was writing before Darwin and he believed that his experiments proved that species were fixed. The process of fertilization had not been understood yet and he thought that several pollen grains fertilized the ovary. Cell theory had not been defined yet either, so Kölreuter decided that the process of fertilization was a blending of juices.

Kölreuter concluded from his experiments that hybrids did not breed true and, therefore, could not be new species.

Herbert and Lecoq

The second man mentioned by Mendel in the introduction to his 1866 paper was William Herbert (1778–1847), a British lawyer and botanist. Herbert was interested in the improvement of cultivated flowers and vegetables.

Herbert read Kölreuter's work and recognized its importance. He crossed lilies to get new garden varieties and he crossed turnips to improve their cropping qualities. Herbert found that the offspring of crosses between two varieties were often bigger and hardier than either of the parents. Turnip hybrids resembled one parent or the other. They were not intermediates.

Herbert referred to Kölreuter as "the father" of hybridization experiments. He realized that Kölreuter's experiments had been neglected. "They do not seem to have been at all followed up by others or to have attracted the attention of cultivators or botanists as they ought to have done." Like Kölreuter, Herbert was interested in the species problem.

The problem, as Herbert saw it, was a matter of words.

Most botanists of the time believed that, if a cross between two plants that looked different gave rise to fertile offspring under natural conditions, then it proved that the two parents were varieties of the same species. If the offspring from the cross were sterile, then it proved that the parents were from different species. If the cross could only be brought about with man's help, then that, too, proved they

A REVOLUTIONARY THEORY

In 1859, the British scientist Charles Darwin (1809–82) published *On the Origin of Species.* In this groundbreaking work, he laid out his theory of natural selection as the process by which new species appear. Darwin recognized that individual characteristics of an organism—its height, strength, ability to react quickly, or to stay hidden— were vitally important in determining whether or not it would survive and have offspring. The better an organism was adapted to its environment, the better its chances would be of surviving to pass on its advantages. Over a long period of time, mutations—changes that are beneficial to an organism—can eventually lead to the evolution of a new species.

Charles Darwin

were separate species.

Herbert maintained that, if two plants could be crossed by any means at all to produce offspring, either fertile or sterile, then those two plants were varieties of the same species. Varieties graded into species and it became a matter of convenience where the line was drawn between them.

"Any discrimination," Herbert wrote in 1837, "between species and permanent varieties of plants is artificial, capricious and insignificant; that the question which is perpetually agitated, whether such a wild plant is a new species, or a variety

Without doubt, *The Origin of Species* changed the world. It started arguments that have lasted until the present day. For many it challenged the teachings of the Bible and threatened religious beliefs. In 1871, Darwin took the argument further when he published *The Descent of Man*, in which he showed that humans had evolved from other forms of life.

One element of natural selection that Darwin could not explain, however, was how beneficial mutations and characteristics were passed on to the next generation. Darwin, like most people of his time, believed characteristics of the parents were blended. Gregor Mendel, who read Darwin's book with great interest, disagreed with this idea. Mendel's research on heredity—which Darwin never had an opportunity to read—would provide a better answer to this question.

of a known species, is waste of intellect on a point which is capable of no precise definition."

Mendel's third reference to a predecessor in plant hybridization was to Henri Lecoq (1802–71), director of the Botanic Garden at Clermont-Ferrand in France. Lecoq was interested in the techniques of hybridization experiments. "However small the corner of the earth may be which a garden amateur can command," Lecoq wrote in 1845, "he is nevertheless in a position to institute a number of useful investigations and noteworthy experiments." He believed that all crop plants could be improved by hybridization and expressed surprise that no one had bred new and more productive varieties of wheat or corn.

Lecoq left detailed descriptions of the practical side of artificial fertilization and he observed, as Kölreuter had done, that "one has almost the certainty of getting many double flowers, as soon as one of the crossed species has become double, and in no wise was the doubleness of both parents necessary as many gardeners believe."

A Major Influence

Mendel's most important reference was to Karl Friedrich von Gärtner (1772–1850). Gärtner was a doctor in the village of Calw in the Black Forest about thirty-seven miles (sixty kilometers) southeast of Stuttgart. He was the son of a famous botanist who had been a friend of Kölreuter and who had allowed Kölreuter to use his garden for some of his hybridization experiments. When his father died in 1791, Gärtner completed his father's work on the fruiting and seeding of plants.

As a result of this work, Gärtner became fascinated by the problems of hybridization. He decided to investigate these problems. Gärtner inquired into the nature of fertilization in plants and the inheritance of seed color.

From 1820 to 1840, Gärtner hybridized plants. In 1830, the Dutch Academy of Sciences offered a prize for an answer to the question: *What does experience teach regarding the production of new species and varieties, through the artificial fertilization of flowers of the one with the pollen of the other and what economic and ornamental plants can be produced and multiplied in this way?*

In 1835, Gärtner sent a summary of his work to the secretary of the academy. The academy accepted the entry and Gärtner set about producing a detailed account of his work. In 1837, Gärtner's treatise of 200 pages with 150 hybrid plant specimens won the prize. The treatise was revised and extended to appear, in 1845, with the title *Experiments and Observations on Hybridization in the Plant Kingdom.*

Gärtner's book contained the results of 10,000 experiments in plant hybridization, and it was from this book that Mendel obtained the "very valuable observations" of his predecessors in plant hybridization. Mendel's copy of the book is heavily underlined and annotated.

Karl Friedrich von Gärtner was a pioneer in the study of hybrids.

Gärtner classified his hybrids into three types: intermediate, commingled, and definite.

The intermediate type was when a precise balance existed between the fertilizing materials of the parents to produce uniform hybrids. The commingled type was intermediate except that the hybrids might show more characters of one parent than the other. The definite type was when the hybrid resembled only one parent.

Gärtner studied variations in both maize (Zea mays, better known as corn) and pea plants. His work inspired Gregor Mendel.

Gärtner accounted for his results in terms of the balance of juices. He assumed that one parent's juice might not blend with the other or that the pollen might produce more juice than the ovary. Gärtner, like Kölreuter, did not understand the process of fertilization.

"The general similarity of hybrids with their stem parents," Gärtner wrote, "can be understood by thinking of the seeds as arising from the mixing which occurs in reproduction and not from the pollen alone. However, since very few hybrids show an equal mixing of the characters of both types, but the one factor in the union often preponderates over the other, so the question arises: which laws govern these modifications in the construction of hybrids?"

Gärtner tried to discover the influence of pollen on seed color in hybrids.

He kept four stocks of maize. One was short with small yellow seeds and the others were tall with large seeds. The large seeds were either brown, red or red-striped. Gärtner tried to cross the short stock with the tall varieties. In 1824, he succeeded with the pollen from the red-striped variety. He got one fertile hybrid plant with five big yellow seeds. The five seeds were sown and Gärtner got four hybrid plants that set seeds. Two had only yellow seeds. One had 224 yellow seeds and 64 red seeds. The other had 104 yellow seeds and 39 red seeds.

Yellow seed to red seed occurred in the proportion of 328 to 103, or a ratio of 3.18 to 1.

Gärtner worked with the garden pea Pisum sativum and recorded the results in the first generation of crossing different varieties. He found that, when he fertilized six flowers of the creeping pea (yellow seeds) with the pollen of the early green brockel pea (blue-green seeds), he obtained 22 seeds, all of which were yellow. He went on to the second hybrid generation by leaving the plants from the 22 seeds to self-fertilize. He obtained some yellow seeds and some blue-green seeds. "The above-mentioned change in color of the seeds of Pisum sativum through hybrid fertilization," Gärtner wrote, "comes out in the second generation more definitely and more decidedly than in the first immediate hybrid product through the immediate influence of the foreign pollen, whereby a quite similar relation as in Mays [maize] and other seeds is produced."

In contrast to the maize experiments, Gärtner did not record the numbers of yellow and blue-green seeds he got in the second hybrid generation of pea crosses. But he had observed dominant characters in seed colors. Yellow in maize and in the pea had obscured the other colors in the first generation hybrid. But, like Kölreuter, Gärtner merely observed it and recorded the 3 to 1 ratio for seed color in second-generation maize hybrids.

Like Kölreuter, Gärtner believed in juices. Not only that at fertilization male and female juices blended to give character, but also that more than one pollen grain was responsible for fertilization of the ovary.

Like Herbert, Gärtner tried to define a species. But Gärtner believed in the "essentiality" of the species. Varieties that were fertile with one another could not as such be thought of as separate species. There was, according to Gärtner, a "specific form" and a "definite sexual relationship" between species.

Gärtner also believed in the fixity of species. The infertility of tobacco plant hybrids was proof of this fixity. "Form and essence," according to Gärtner, "are in this connection one."

A Better Understanding of Fertilization

Mendel's final reference in his introduction is to another German hybridizer, Max Ernst Wichura (1817–66). Wichura was a botanist in Breslau. In 1865, he published the results of the work he had been doing on the willow *Salix*. He did not study individual characters of plants, as Gärtner had done, but crossed different species of willow and studied the plants as a whole. He found that many hybrids were bigger and more vigorous than the parental types.

Wichura's hybrids were usually intermediate between the parents. "In hybrid fertilization, if unlike factors unite, there arises an intermediate formation." The same result was obtained whichever parent provided the pollen because "constant characters, through which the parent species are distinguished from one another, go half over to the hybrid so that it holds the middle position between them." Wichura's idea of fertilization was more precise than either Kölreuter's or Gärtner's had been.

In referring to reciprocal crosses, Wichura states that it follows "with mathematical certainty, that the pollen cell must have exactly the same share in the conformation of the fertilization product as the egg." His writings reflect the growing influence of the cell theory on the interpretation of the process of fertilization.

Mendel had studied under Franz Unger at Vienna, and Unger was a supporter

A honey bee with pollen grains on its body emerges from a flower. The process of fertilization was not well understood in Mendel's time.

of the 1838 cell theory of Schleiden. Schleiden believed that cells were the basis of all living organisms. But Schleiden was unable to interpret the process of fertilization.

Many years before the cell theory, Italian microscopist Jean-Baptista Amici (1784–1860) had been able to study a single pollen grain and had watched it put out a projection. In 1830, with an improved microscope, he was able to see the projection from the pollen grow as a tube down the style of a female plant to reach and make contact with the ovary. Watching this in orchids and gourds, he was convinced that only one pollen tube ever grew down to the egg cell and he was also convinced that the pollen tube never penetrated the egg cell. He explained what he saw in the conventional manner of the time: Juice leaked from the end of the pollen tube through the membranes of the ovary to blend with the juices of the egg cell.

Schleiden was opposed to the idea of juices. He was also opposed to the idea of equal contribution by male and female. He thought the beginning of the new plant, the plant **embryo**, was formed from the tip of the pollen tube where it pushed into the wall of the embryo sac. The embryo sac provided only nourishment for the embryo to develop. He would not accept that there could be a fusion of male pollen and female egg cell elements in spite of the growing evidence of the plant hybridizers.

In 1856, Nathaniel Pringsheim (1823–94) saw fertilization in the freshwater alga *Oedogonium*. One **spermatozoon** went into one egg cell. In 1856, a pupil of Schleiden's saw the pollen tube **nucleus** enter the embryo sac and fuse with the egg cell nucleus.

Schleiden was at last convinced that male and female plants contribute equally to the offspring by the fusion of cells.

In 1856, Mendel began his experiments.

TEXT-DEPENDENT QUESTIONS

1. What type of plant did Joseph Gottlieb Kölreuter study initially?
2. What did William Herbert determine about species?
3. Where did Karl Friedrich von Gärtner conduct his experiments?
4. What did Max Ernst Wichura learn about willow hybrds?

RESEARCH PROJECT

When Charles Darwin published his theory of natural selection in 1859, he created an uproar. To this day, the subject of evolution provokes debate in many communities. Using the local library or the internet, find out about some important court cases that deal with the teaching of evolution and its religious-based alternatives, such as creationism or intelligent design. These could include the 1925 Scopes trial in Tennessee, or more recent federal court cases like *Webster v. New Lenox School District* (1990) or *Kitzmiller v. Dover* (2005). Do some research on both sides of the case, and write a two-page summary that can be presented to your class.

Mendel chose the garden pea plant (Pisum sativum) because it was easy to fertilize and many varieties were available to be grown in his garden. When crossbreeding different varieties, he found that purple flowers, such as the ones shown here, were dominant over white flowers.

WORDS TO UNDERSTAND

apomixis—reproduction without the fusion of germ cells.

floret—one of a cluster of small flowers that make a flower head, as in hawkweeds and dandelions.

genotype—all the genes of a particular plant or animal.

keel—the two lower petals of flowers of the pea family that form an envelope around the reproductive parts of the flower.

phenotype—the appearance of a plant or animal resulting from the interaction of its genes and its surroundings.

CHAPTER 4

Mendel's Experiments

Cell theory and 100 years of experimental hybridization had shown that male and female plants contribute equally to their offspring. Plant hybridizers had studied single characters and recorded dominance. Gärtner had counted colored maize seeds of the second generation. But no unifying principle of inheritance had been found.

Mendel brought the techniques of physics to the study of plant breeding. The laws of chance and of probability were applied to the process of fertilization. Two cells fuse to give one cell. "It remains, therefore, purely a matter of chance," Mendel wrote, "which of the two sorts of pollen will become united with each separate egg cell."

Designs and methods from physical experiments were brought into biology. Mendel intended to count the results of hybrid crosses, which required planned experiments. "Not one [previous experiment by plant hybridizers] had been carried out to such an extent and in such a way," Mendel wrote, "as to make it possible to determine the number of different forms under which the offspring of hybrids appear, or to arrange these forms with certainty according to their separate generations or definitely to ascertain their statistical relations."

Choosing the Pea Plant

A suitable plant was required that had easily controlled self-fertilization and cross-fertilization so that there should be no difficulty in bringing about one

The brothers of Saint Thomas's Abbey in the early 1860s. Mendel is standing in the back, second from the right, holding a fuchsia, his favorite flower. Abbot Cyril Franz Napp is seated in front of Mendel, with a cross around his neck and a book in his hands.

or the other according to the plan of the experiment. It must be easy to protect the flowers from unwanted pollen. Mendel chose the pea family because of the structure of its flowers.

The stamens and style are packed inside the **keel**, formed from the fusion of the two lower petals. Self-fertilization takes place inside this package before the flower opens. Self-fertilization, therefore, usually occurs before there is any possibility of pollen from other plants reaching the stigma.

Cross-fertilization would be done by hand. "For this purpose," Mendel wrote, "the bud is opened before it is perfectly developed, the keel is removed and each stamen carefully extracted by means of forceps, after which the stigma can at once be dusted over with the foreign pollen." The flowers would then be covered with a bag.

From among the plants that have this type of flower in the pea family, Mendel selected the garden pea *Pisum sativum*. Many varieties were obtainable and they were easy to grow. The peas were grown on a small garden plot behind the monastery building. To keep several experiments going at the same time, the plants were crammed together, growing over the fence and up trees. When there was no more room on the plot, which was the only part of the garden he was allowed to use for his experiments, the peas could be grown in pots.

Plants suitable for Mendel's experiments had to have conspicuous characters that stayed constant in self-fertilizing lines. Each variety of pea was cultivated and allowed to self-fertilize for two years. All but one remained constant, where each generation was like the last. Mendel had established pure lines that proved not to vary.

In Mendel's time, this was the floor of the greenhouse at St. Thomas's Abbey in Brno. Mendel grew some pea plants in the greenhouse, so they would not be cross-fertilized by bees or other insects, thus contaminating his experiments.

From thirty-four varieties of pea, Mendel selected twenty-two that had characteristics that were easy to study. During the period of experiments, from 1856 to 1863, the twenty-two varieties were allowed to grow and self-fertilize. Thus, Mendel always had a standard to which he could compare the results of his artificial crossings.

Plants grown in a greenhouse served as controls for the outdoor crosses. Bees and weevils could be kept out of the greenhouse so there was no risk of cross-fertilization by these animals. This was the first time that experiments in plant hybridization had been planned in this way.

Plants suitable for Mendel's experiments had to have contrasting characters. He found several characters of form and size and color that had simple alternatives in the pure breeding lines. Mendel selected fifteen characters but, finally, reduced the number to the seven that showed the clearest contrasts.

He found it difficult to make a decision between a small pea and a big pea, a small leaf and a big leaf because, as he wrote, "the difference is of a *more* or *less* nature." He rejected the "more or less" characters and chose instead to study color and form of flowers, pods, and seeds. Length of stem was also included because it proved not to be a "more or less" character. Long-stemmed plants were six times taller than short-stemmed plants.

Mendel's Experiments

Mendel crossed plants with purple flowers and brown seed coats with plants with white flowers and white seed coats after proving that the color of the seed coat and of the flowers was always the same on the one plant.

He crossed plants with flowers evenly distributed along the stalk with plants with flowers clustered at the tip. He crossed plants with smooth seeds with plants with wrinkled seeds. He crossed plants with yellow or orange seeds with plants with seeds of a "more or less intense green tint." He crossed plants with fat pods with plants with shrunk pods. He crossed plants with green pods with plants with yellow or red pods. He crossed plants with long stems (over six feet) and plants with short stems (under three feet).

When Mendel crossbred tall and short pea plant varieties, he found that in the first generation, all the offspring were just as tall, on average, as the original tall plants. To explain this, Mendel determined that among pea plants, "tall" was a dominant characteristic and "short" was a recessive characteristic.

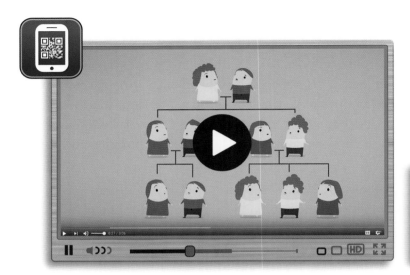

Scan here for a video about Mendel's pea plant experiments:

Mendel used only the plants in which the characters were conspicuous and contrasting. He always made two sets of crosses: one variety provided the pollen for the first cross; the other variety provided it for the second.

Mendel said that he knew already from what he had seen of ornamental plants that hybrids are not always exactly intermediate between the parents. They may, for example, be intermediate in the form and size of the leaves, but in other characteristics, one of the two parental characters is "preponderant." Mendel now showed that in none of his crosses with the seven selected characteristics were the offspring intermediate between the parents.

Mendel proposed to call the characteristic that preponderated the dominant characteristic and the other, that did not show in the hybrids, the recessive.

He selected plants for the experiments that showed clear dominance relationships. He had, in fact, purposely rejected those characteristics, such as size of seed and leaf, that showed a range of intermediacy in the hybrids.

When Mendel crossed a plant with purple flowers with a plant with white flowers, all the offspring had purple flowers. It did not matter which was the pollen-producing plant. Purple was dominant to white. There were no intermediate plants with pink flowers.

Kölreuter had seen this in his crosses of double and single *Dianthus* plants. Gärtner's yellow-seed maize was dominant to his red-seed maize. But Kölreuter and Gärtner had observed and recorded only unrelated facts.

Of the other six characteristics, Mendel found that even distribution of flowers was dominant to clustered. The smooth pea was dominant to the wrinkled pea and the yellow pea to the green pea. The fat pod was dominant to the shrunken pod and the green pod to the yellow pod. Finally, Mendel found that the tall stem was dominant to the short stem.

Herbert had observed that his hybrid turnips were bigger and hardier than the parents. Wichura's hybrid willows were bigger and more vigorous. Mendel observed that the hybrid between a tall plant and a short plant was often taller than the tall parent.

Mendel found that the smooth pea is dominant; the wrinkled pea, recessive.

In *Experiments in Plant Hybridization*, Mendel described these experiments and concluded that Kölreuter and Gärtner were wrong in saying that almost all first-generation hybrids were intermediate between the two parents. "Transitional forms," he wrote, "were not observed in any experiment." Instead, Mendel argued that one characteristic was usually dominant to the other and the hybrid, therefore, resembled only one of its parents.

Continuing the Experiments

Mendel continued to the second generation. The hybrid from a cross between a plant with smooth peas and one with wrinkled peas had smooth peas only. Mendel let 253 smooth pea hybrids self-fertilize. The result was 7,324 peas. Mendel found that 5,474 of the peas were smooth but 1,850 were wrinkled.

Smooth was dominant to wrinkled and all the F^1 generation hybrids had smooth peas. But in the F^2 generation the wrinkled peas turned up again. In the experiment the count gave a proportion of 2.96 smooth peas to 1 wrinkled.

Other hybrid self-fertilizations gave similar results in the F^2 generation. Yellow peas occurred in the proportion of 3.01 dominant yellow peas to 1 recessive green pea. Measuring the height of the plants resulted in 787 tall pea plants and 277 short plants, a ratio of 2.84 to 1. Mendel found that 705 plants with purple flowers occurred with 224 plants with white flowers, a ratio of 3.15 to 1.

Mendel therefore discovered that the constant relationship between the dominant and recessive characteristics in the second hybrid generation was a ratio of about 3 to 1. Out of every four plants, three would exhibit the dominant characteristic, and one would show the recessive. Mendel concluded that the characteristics "must pass over [from one generation to the next] unchanged."

The next stage was to see what happened when the plants of the second hybrid generation self-fertilized.

The hybrids that showed the recessive characteristic bred true. All the offspring had green peas or were short or had white flowers. But only one third of the dominant characteristic bearing plants bred true.

The yellow-pea hybrids and the tall hybrids and the purple-flower hybrids bred

After Mendel's death, British geneticist Reginald Punnett developed a way to show the likely outcome of crossbreeding of hybrids when the dominant and recessive characteristics are known. The diagram is called a Punnett square. In pea flowers, Mendel found that the purple color is dominant (B) and white color recessive (b). Breeding two hybrid plants, which would both have purple flowers (Bb), results in three plants with purple flowers (BB, Bb, and Bb) and one that exhibits the recessive white color (bb).

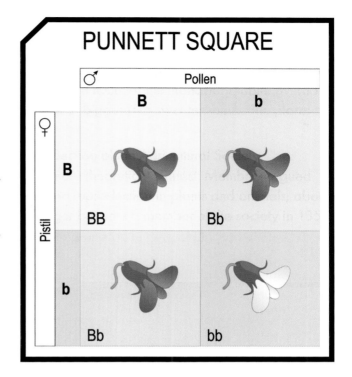

one-third true. The other two-thirds of the plants behaved like the hybrids of the F^1 generation, producing plants that followed the 3 to 1 ratio of dominant to recessive characteristics.

Understanding Mendel's Findings

Mendel confirmed the findings of Gärtner and Kölreuter that hybrids often revert to the parental forms, but Mendel's interpretation of the results was revolutionary.

To explain his results, he considered each of the characteristics as a unitary unchanging characteristic. "If A be taken as denoting one of the two constant characteristics, for instance, the dominant, a the recessive, and Aa the hybrid form in which both are conjoined, the expression A + 2Aa + a shows the terms in the series of progeny of the hybrids of two differentiating characteristics." The hybrid Aa possesses both the characteristics of the parents but appears to be only like the parent with the dominant characteristic.

He then argued that the hybrid produces pollen or egg cells that are either A or a and in equal numbers. "In the opinion of renowned physiologists, for the purpose of propagation one pollen cell and one egg cell unite in phanerogams [plants that produce seeds] into a single cell, which is capable of assimilation and formation of new cells to become an independent organism." He supposed that it would be entirely a matter of chance whether an A pollen grain fertilized an A egg cell or an a egg cell.

Mendel not only explained the facts of hybridization through three generations but also confirmed mathematically that the contributions of pollen and egg cell were equal. He suggested that characteristics occur in pairs, with dominance relations to one another. He decided on mathematical grounds that each parent passes on only one of its two characteristics to its offspring and this characteristic combines with only one of the characteristics of the other parent.

This is called Mendel's First Law or the Law of Segregation. The revolutionary part of this work was to suggest unchanging factors existing in pairs, but which segregated (separated) from one another so that only one characteristic of the pair was contained in the pollen grain and only one in the egg cell. The two single characteristics then united to generate the pairs for the next generation. The characteristics from the two parents did not blend nor alter one another in any way. They were there unchanged and ready to segregate again to give new combinations in the F^2 generation.

Which characteristic combines with which at fertilization is a matter of chance, but according to "the laws of probability," Mendel wrote, "it will always happen, on the average of many cells, that each pollen from A and a will unite equally often with each egg cell from A and a." By the operation of the law of chance, the types will appear in the F^2 generation in the proportion of $AA + 2Aa + aa$, or three apparent dominant types to one recessive.

In 1861, Mendel tried crossing plants that differed from one another in more than one characteristic. Again, he did not find intermediate forms. He crossed plants that had smooth peas which were yellow with plants that had wrinkled seeds which were green. The first generation were all with smooth and yellow peas because these two characteristics are dominant. When he allowed eighteen of these hybrids to self-fertilize, he managed to get 556 peas. Of those, 315 were smooth and yellow, 101 were wrinkled and yellow, 108 were smooth and green and 32 were wrinkled and green.

From this, Mendel concluded that the characteristics were segregating and combining independently of one another because this ratio for two characteristics, 9 + 3 + 3+ 1, is the product of the simple multiplication of the results from each pair of characteristics separately (3 + 1) x (3 + 1). This finding is known as Mendel's Second Law, or the Law of Independent Assortment.

Informing the Public

In 1865, Mendel talked about his results to the Brno Natural History Society. The local newspaper reported the "interesting" work. Society members, local teachers, and doctors, were stimulated to a brief discussion.

In addition to peas, Mendel talked about beans and *Dianthus* plants. He found that white-flower or red-flower *Dianthus caryophyllus* bred true. Mendel had crossed runner beans *Phaseolus multiflorus* and French beans *Phaseolus vulgaris* with the bush bean *Phaseolus nanus*. In beans, Mendel showed that height, pod color, and pod form were characteristics inherited in exactly the same way as in pea plants. But flower color proved difficult. Mendel was puzzled because a cross between a plant with red flowers and one with white flowers resulted in offspring with flowers that were a paler red than the red parent.

When Mendel let this F^1 generation self-fertilize, the F^2 gave every variety of flower color from red to white. Pure white was rare. Mendel suggested that flower color in beans must be controlled by more than one characteristic.

Mendel assumed that all hybrid plants should follow the rules for *Pisum*. Gärtner's intermediate hybrids, he believed, could be the result either of studying many characteristics at the same time, not all of which were dominant in the same parent; the result of not making pure lines first; or the result of having features which, like the bean flower colors, were the result of several interacting characteristics. Much of the confusion in hybrid crosses, according to Mendel, was because in the F^2 generation the apparent dominant characteristics did not all behave in the same way when self-fertilized. He distinguished two types among the apparent dominants.

Mendel was the first to distinguish between the outward appearance of a plant (now called the **phenotype**) and the inward composition (now called the **genotype**). The three dominant purple-flower peas of the F^2 generation were all of the same phenotype. They were not all of the same genotype. One-third had two like characteristics (PP). The other two-thirds had two unlike characteristics (Pp).

Mendel realized that large numbers are needed to give meaningful results. The number required increases as the number of characteristics being studied increases. Mendel criticized Gärtner for not having used enough plants in his crosses.

Mendel did not think that either Gärtner or Kölreuter had proved by their experiments that species were fixed. Neither did he think that his own experiments proved that they were not. But "changes of type must take place if the conditions of life be altered and the species possesses the capacity of fitting itself to its new environment," he wrote. Like Herbert, Mendel thought that species and varieties graded into one another.

"It has so far been found," Mendel wrote, "to be just as impossible to draw a sharp line between hybrids of species and varieties as between species and varieties themselves."

In 1866, Mendel's contribution to the Brno Natural History Society was published. Mendel received forty reprints of *Experiments on Plant Hybridization*, as his paper was called. He is known to have sent out several copies, one of which went to Karl Wilhelm von Nägeli.

A Challenging Problem

Nägeli (1817–91) had worked with Schleiden in Jena and had shown that cells were formed from other cells by dividing in half and not by budding, as Schleiden and others believed. In 1865, Nägeli had published a review of the work of Kölreuter and Gärtner. Nägeli agreed with Mendel, rather than with the others, that there was no great difference between species and varieties, except that varieties were more like one another and tended to be more fertile. But he followed Kölreuter and Gärtner in thinking that the F^1 generation was the result of an unknown type of mixing of the parent characteristics to create a new hybrid characteristic.

Further, Nägeli believed that all the individuals of later generations must be variable. There was no suggestion in his mind that half the F^2 generation could breed true (either for the dominant characteristics or the recessives). When Nägeli received Mendel's paper, he could not believe that Mendel had found the answer to the inheritance of characteristics in plant hybrids.

Nägeli believed that all hybrid plants of both F^1 and F^2 generations would have both

Versuche über Pflanzen-Hybriden.

Von

Gregor Mendel.

(Vorgelegt in den Sitzungen vom 8. Februar und 8. März 1865.)

Einleitende Bemerkungen.

Künstliche Befruchtungen, welche an Zierpflanzen desshalb vorgenommen wurden, um neue Farben-Varianten zu erzielen, waren die Veranlassung zu den Versuchen, die her besprochen werden sollen. Die auffallende Regelmässigkeit, mit welcher dieselben Hybridformen immer wiederkehrten, so oft die Befruchtung zwischen gleichen Arten geschah, gab die Anregung zu weiteren Experimenten, deren Aufgabe es war, die Entwicklung der Hybriden in ihren Nachkommen zu verfolgen.

Dieser Aufgabe haben sorgfältige Beobachter, wie Kölreuter, Gärtner, Herbert, Lecocq, Wichura u. a. einen Theil ihres Lebens mit unermüdlicher Ausdauer geopfert. Namentlich hat Gärtner in seinem Werke „die Bastarderzeugung im Pflanzenreiche" sehr schätzbare Beobachtungen niedergelegt, und in neuester Zeit wurden von Wichura gründliche Untersuchungen über die Bastarde der Weiden veröffentlicht. Wenn es noch nicht gelungen ist, ein allgemein giltiges Gesetz für die Bildung und Entwicklung der Hybriden aufzustellen, so kann das Niemanden Wunder nehmen, der den Umfang der Aufgabe kennt und die Schwierigkeiten zu würdigen weiss, mit denen Versuche dieser Art zu kämpfen haben. Eine endgiltige Entscheidung kann erst dann erfolgen, bis Detail Versuche aus den verschiedensten Pflanzen-Familien vorliegen. Wer die Ar-

1*

First page of the manuscript of Mendel's Experiments in Plant Hybridization, *published in 1866. The work would attract little interest over the next thirty-five years.*

A and a in their bodies, and sooner or later, this hybrid condition would show itself. Nägeli was working with plants in the genus *Hieracium*, commonly known as hawkweed, and his hybrids bred true. Of course, his reply to Mendel's paper was to suggest that Mendel should do some work with *Hieracium*.

The hawkweeds are very difficult to cross because of the arrangement of the reproductive parts of the flower. Each **floret** has a fine tube, formed by the fusion of the stamens, through which the style passes. It needs delicate dissection and good eyesight to remove the stamens without damaging the style.

Mendel tried to improve the lighting conditions for this operation by using an artificial light source with a lens and mirrors but suffered severe eye strain.

Mendel worked on breeding and crossing *Hieracium* for five years, from 1866 to 1871, but he could not get the same results as he had got with *Pisum*. Most of his crosses were a failure. When he did succeed in making fertile hybrids, they bred true, to his surprise. In 1869, Mendel read a paper on *Hieracium* to the Brno Natural History Society.

He could not explain his results, but it is clear that he still considered that *Pisum* illustrated the usual way of inheritance and that *Hieracium*, like the willows of Wichura, showed "peculiar behavior of their hybrids." In this, Mendel was correct.

Hawkweed is an example of a plant that reproduces by **apomixis**. That is to say, the pollen only stimulates the egg cell to develop; it does not fuse with it. This makes it difficult to achieve crosses in the first place and, because there is no fertilization in the normal reproductive process, the hybrids do indeed breed true.

It is not surprising that Mendel was unable to explain *Hieracium*, nor is it very surprising that Nägeli thought Mendel was wrong about the F^2 hybrid generation showing segregation into pure types like the P^1 generation and hybrid types like the F^1.

From a piece of paper with Mendel's writing on it, it is known that he was still trying to work out a common law of heredity for the *Hieracium*, *Salix* and *Pisum* results in the late 1870s. But by that time, he had many other pressing issues to deal with, and not as much time for further contributions to biological theory.

1. What are some of the reasons why Mendel chose to experiment with pea plants?
2. What were the characteristics that Mendel sought to study in peas?
3. What is a dominant characteristic? What is a recessive characteristic?
4. In what ratio did Mendel find dominant to recessive characteristics in second-generation hybrids?

RESEARCH PROJECT

Visit the website of the National Human Genome Research Institute (www.genome.gov) to find out more about this organization and its purpose. Write a two-page paper and present it to the class.

chromosome—threads in the nucleus of all cells that contain genetic information. The number of chromosomes is usually constant for each species.

cytoplasm—the substance of the cell, excluding the nucleus, composed of a complex of membranes.

gamete—the germ cells that unite to form a new cell from which the offspring develops.

gemmule—particles once thought to be made in all parts of the body and sent to the germ cells for passing on to the next generation.

germ cell—the cells that unite to form a new cell from which the offspring develops.

heterozygous—having paired unlike genes.

meiosis—a division of the nucleus in which the number of chromosomes is halved.

mitosis—a division of the nucleus that results in two identical new nuclei with the same number of chromosomes as the original.

zygote—the cell formed from the fusion of male and female germ cells from which the embryo develops.

CHAPTER 5

Mendel the Abbot

In 1868, the local newspaper of Brno announced the election of a new abbot. Abbot Napp had died, and the twelve brothers of the monastery elected Mendel to succeed him. "The population," the local newspaper reported, "greets the election with undivided joy."

In a letter to Nägeli, Mendel expressed the hope that, as abbot, he would have more time and, more importantly, more space to conduct his experiments.

He resigned from teaching at the technical school. But, as abbot of a rich and influential monastery, Mendel was expected to play a part in local politics. He did this so well that in 1872, Mendel was made Commander of the Order of Franz Joseph for his "meritorious and patriotic activities" as abbot.

In Austrian politics, Mendel supported the German Liberal Party. When the Party was asked to propose a chairman for the Moravian Mortgage Bank, Mendel was appointed. The chairmanship meant daily duties at the bank. Mendel was also elected to committees on education, on roads, and on agriculture. At the same time, as abbot, Mendel had to manage the monastery estates and visit nearby farms. Mendel now had the entire monastery garden for his experiments, but he had less time.

Changing Focus

Until 1871, Mendel went on with the *Hieracium* experiments. The experiments were difficult and the results unsatisfactory. Finally, increasing calls on his time persuaded him to abandon *Hieracium*.

Mendel's 1868 election as abbott, or head of the monastery in Brno, made it difficult for him to continue with his experiments in heredity.

Mendel made few further planned experiments, but he did satisfy himself with fertilization experiments with the *Mirabilis jalapa* (Marvel of Peru) plant, showing that one pollen grain was enough for fertilization. He saw that fertilization was often more successful if there were a number of grains on the stigma. Mendel put this down to a rivalry that existed between the grains so that only the most vigorous succeeded.

Mendel's scientific work became a leisure activity.

He set up colonies of bees and designed a fertilization cage to control crosses between bees of different varieties. He obtained bees from Italy, southern Austria, and Cyprus, as well as South American bees that arrived in Moravia with a load of timber. He gave lectures to the Brno Natural History Society on beekeeping and breeding.

Mendel observed that a hive from which the queen had been taken rears more of its own queens, even if supplied immediately with a queen of another variety. Mendel studied the inheritance of the industry of the hive, flight characteristics, bee color, and aggressiveness. Unfortunately, none of Mendel's research notes on bees have survived. It has been suggested that one of Mendel's aims was to test the observation, made in 1854, that the drones produced by a hybrid queen resemble either of her parents but are never intermediate.

Mendel grafted and hybridized fruit trees and flowers. By crossbreeding, he produced pear strains that ripened at different times of the year. He displayed the results of his breeding experiments at local agricultural shows. He won prizes and a fuchsia plant was even named after him. The "Prelate Mendel" was "very large, pale blue shading into violet, luxuriant, regular structure, sepals light, very beautiful, blooms early." The fuchsia was Mendel's favorite flower and he put one into his coat of arms.

Every day, Mendel made recordings of air pressure, temperature, and hours of sunshine. He summed up the material in monthly graphs. He also studied sunspots. In a paper submitted to the Brno Natural History Society, he concluded that there was a relation between sunspot activity and the northern lights (*aurora borealis*), as well as a relation between the eleven-year sunspot cycle and the

The colorful fuchsia plant was Mendel's favorite, and one variety was even named after him.

weather. Others had held similar ideas, but in Mendel's time they were largely rejected. However, more than a century later, scientists had developed a better understanding of the relationship between sunspots and the earth's magnetic field. A 2009 study by researchers from the National Center for Atmospheric Research concluded that the sunspot cycle has a major effect on the earth's weather.

During the 1870s Mendel's health deteriorated, in part because he became involved in a political dispute. The Austrian government proposed a heavy tax on Church property to raise money to support parish priests. The monastery of Brno refused to pay. Mendel felt that the State was interfering in the internal affairs of Rome. He exhausted himself with ten years of legal battles over the tax.

On January 6, 1884, Mendel died of Bright's disease: chronic deterioration of the kidneys. "His death," the local newspaper reported, "deprives the poor of a benefactor and mankind at large of a man of the noblest character, one who was a warm friend, a promoter of the natural sciences and an exemplary priest."

Mendel's Impact on Genetic Theory

There were no immediate successors to Mendel. In fact, during his lifetime, Mendel's paper aroused little interest.

In 1866, the Brno Natural History Society sent six copies of its *Transactions* to Vienna, eight to Berlin, four to the United States, and two to England. Some of Mendel's reprints have been traced. He sent one to Holland, one to Austrian botanist Anton Kerner von Marilaun (1831–98), and two to Germany, one of which was the copy to Nägeli in Munich. Nägeli was not prepared to publicize Mendel's experiments because they did not explain the results of his own experiments. Authors of books on plant hybridization were mainly interested in the hawkweed paper. No one suspected that Mendel's results had universal application.

But Mendel's mathematical approach to plant hybridization had provided a vigorous new theory. Hereditary units, or particles, exist in pairs. Each unit separates from its partner and passes by itself into a **germ cell**. This is known as segregation. When male and female germ cells fuse in sexual reproduction, each unit pairs with a new partner and this is known as recombination.

In 1866, there was no physical basis for supposing that characteristics were in pairs in organisms, nor any basis to account for their segregation.

Also, Mendel had not joined his theory with Charles Darwin's theory of evolution by natural selection. Mendel had read Darwin and believed that a continuous evolutionary process was a possibility and that his own work might have some bearing on the problem of the origin of species. "It requires indeed some courage," he wrote of his experiments, "to undertake a labor of such far-reaching extent; this appears, however, to be the only right way by which we can finally reach the solution of a question the importance of which cannot be overestimated in connection with the history of the evolution of organic forms." Apart from this, Mendel did not enter the discussions on evolution.

There is no evidence that Darwin ever read Mendel's paper. It has been said that if he had, Darwin would have recognized Mendel's importance. The Mendelian theories were what Darwin was looking for as the basis for the variability on which natural selection could work.

But Darwin knew about the inheritance of recessive characteristics. He had made experiments with gray and white mice. The offspring were not piebald or pale gray, but dark gray like one parent and, in the next generation, were either gray or white. He had crossed hairy and smooth plants and the resulting plants were hairy, yet smooth ones turned up again in later generations.

Darwin did not believe that these crosses told him anything relevant to evolutionary theory. The "sports" (white mice, for example) would already have been eliminated by natural selection, and it was only the artificiality of the crosses that caused them to show up again. A hairy plant was often considered to be a different species from a smooth one and species crosses, according to Darwin, were not the sort of changes that occurred naturally. If they did occur, they did not make a new species.

Finally, Darwin believed in blending inheritance, and he also believed that more than one pollen grain grew down the style of a plant to fertilize the egg cell. Blending inheritance depends on the assumptions that each parent

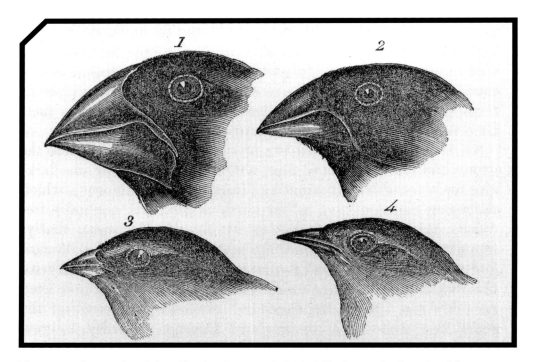

This page from a book by Charles Darwin (1809–82) shows the heads of four finches he discovered in the Galapagos Islands. Darwin realized that each of these different birds had developed from one type of bird that had reached the islands from the mainland. Darwin's 1859 book On the Origin of Species *presented his theory that all living creatures had evolved from a common ancestor, and that differences were due to a process he called "natural selection." Mendel read Darwin's book with great interest.*

contributes equally to the offspring (which agrees with Mendel's theory) and that those contributions are halved at each generation (which does not agree with Mendel's theory). It was Francis Galton (1822–1911), a cousin of Darwin, who worked out blending inheritance, mathematically, in his *Ancestral Law of Inheritance.*

Galton thought he could show, from the statistical analysis of populations, that the parent contributes half its inheritance to the offspring (which agrees with Mendel) but that each grandparent provides a quarter and each great-grandparent an eighth of the inheritance (which does not agree with Mendel).

It can be guessed then that Darwin would not have appreciated fully the importance of Mendel's work for the general theory of evolution. It is perhaps not surprising, therefore, that Darwin's followers did not recognize Mendel's work either.

Slow Recognition

Only three years after the publication of *Experiments in Plant Hybridization*, Mendel's name was recorded in the literature of hybridization. In a book published in Giessen, Germany, in 1869 on the subject of species and varieties, Hermann Hoffmann (1819–91) referred twice to Mendel's work, once to some studies on *Geum* and once to *Pisum*. Of the *Pisum* work, he concluded that Mendel had shown that "hybrids possess an inclination in the following generation to strike back to the parental species."

In 1881, Wilhelm Olbers Focke (1834–1922) published a long work on plant hybridization in which he tried to record all the examples of hybrid plants that had ever been made. He had done some experiments himself on foxgloves and a few other plants and was exceptional in that he recorded the measurements he had made of parts of plants whose inheritance he was studying. He measured the petals and sepals of parent foxgloves and their hybrid offspring and found the hybrid measurements more or less intermediate between the parents. Focke mentions Mendel's work fifteen times but, interestingly, the *Pisum* experiments are mentioned only once, the *Hieracium* work several times. The results of the *Pisum* experiments were not in agreement with other experiments on hundreds of different plants. Thus, finally, Focke considers Mendel's work as no more than "to be designated as particularly instructive" along with that of several other people.

In the same year, Mendel's name was listed among plant hybridizers in an article that George Romanes (1848–94) wrote for the *Encyclopaedia Britannica* on "Hybridism."

In 1895, *Plant Breeding* by Liberty Hyde Bailey (1858–1954) contained no reference to Mendel but, in later editions, quoted the section of Focke's book that referred to Mendel's experiments.

As far as it is known, these were the only references to Mendel's work before 1900.

Hugo de Vries as an old man, looking at two flowers that he is holding close to his chest.

Mendel had been dead for sixteen years when Dutch scientist Hugo de Vries (1848–1935) sent a paper in March 1900 to the Academy of Sciences in Paris called, "On the Law of Segregation in Hybrids." The conclusion of this short paper was that inheritance could be considered as depending on distinct units that segregate from one another in hybrids. "The totality of these experiments establishes the law of segregation of hybrids and confirms the principles that I have expressed concerning the specific characteristics considered as being distinct units," he wrote. Soon afterward, a Dutch friend from the city of Delft sent de Vries a copy of Mendel's paper. "I know that you are studying hybrids," wrote his friend Professor Martinus Willem Beyerinck (1851–1931), "so perhaps the enclosed reprint of the year 1865 of a certain Mendel which I happen to possess is still of some interest to you." Professor Beyerinck recognized the radical importance of Mendel's work and, at that moment, so did de Vries.

In a German-language version of his paper, which he was preparing to send for publication, de Vries hastily altered the conclusion that he had sent to Paris. "From these and many other experiments I conclude that the law of segregation of hybrids in the plant kingdom, which Mendel established for peas, has a very general application and a fundamental significance for the study of the units out of which the specific characteristics are compounded." De Vries described Mendel's paper as *trop beau pour son temps* ("ahead of its time") which accords with Mendel's own disappointed assessment, *mein Zeit wird schon kommen* ("my time will come").

De Vries was more in touch with the scientific world than Mendel had been and sent copies of his German paper to other scientists that he knew it would interest, like Erich von Tschermak and Carl Correns.

In October 1899, Correns (1864–1933) developed the idea of particulate inheritance and, only a few weeks later, picked up a reference to Mendel's paper in Focke's book. This was not the first time he had heard of Mendel, for Correns had been a pupil of Nägeli and Nägeli had mentioned Mendel's work on *Hieracium* but not on peas. In May 1900, an essay by Correns appeared, titled, "G. Mendel's Law of the Behavior of the Progeny of Hybrid Races." In his essay, Correns told the world that both he and de Vries had been preceeded by Mendel.

Tschermak (1871–1962) had chosen to study inheritance in peas and, in 1899, searching through the literature, found a reference in Focke's book to the work of Mendel on *Pisum sativum*. "I had on the same day of this discovery the Transactions of the Natural History Society of Brno hunted out of the University Library, which now gave me the information, to my greatest surprise, that the regular relationships discovered by me, had already been

In 1900, German botanist Carl Correns independently developed a theory of inherited characteristics, then discovered it was similar to the one Mendel had proposed in 1865. In his paper, Correns gave credit for the discovery to Mendel.

discovered by Mendel much earlier." In June 1900, having received his copy of Mendel's article from de Vries, Tschermak published his paper "On Experimental Crosses in *Pisum sativum*."

THOMAS HUNT MORGAN

In 1907 Thomas Hunt Morgan (1866–1945), an American scientist, began a series of experiments using the tiny fruit fly, *Drosophila melanogaster*. The advantages in using *Drosophila* were that it could be kept in large numbers very easily, it bred very quickly, and it only had four pairs of chromosomes. Morgan tried to establish the role of chromosomes by producing mutations in his fruit flies. Hugo de Vries had proposed that every so often, a new variety of an organism might appear that was different in some respect from either of its parents. De Vries called these sudden changes "mutations." Morgan failed to produce mutations artificially, but he did find enough natural examples to be able to carry out his experiments.

By following the mutations from generation to generation, Morgan showed that many characteristics were linked together, and therefore must be on the same chromosome. However, he observed that sometimes the linked characteristics could be inherited separately. It seemed that when the sex cells were being formed, pairs of chromosomes could exchange part of their length with each other so that linked pairs of genes might be split up. The greater the length of chromosome that separated the two genes, the greater was the chance that they would be separated when the chromosomes crossed over and exchanged material. By studying how often various linked pairs were split up, Morgan was able to begin drawing up the first chromosome map, showing roughly where the fruit fly's genes were.

The illustration here shows the results of crossing a white-eyed female

William Bateson (1861–1926) was another scientist who received a reprint of de Vries's German paper. He, too, hunted out the 1866 *Transactions* of the Brno Natural History Society. In May 1900, Bateson lectured to members of the Royal

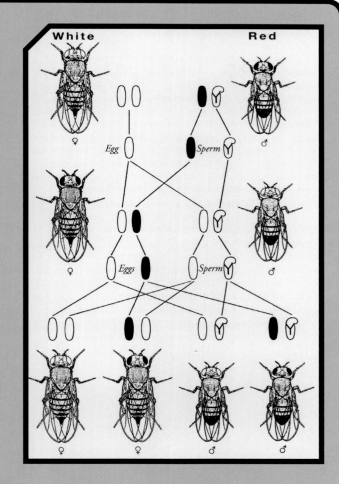

with a red-eyed male. It is very similar to Mendel's pea-crossing experiment. The female can only pass on genes for white eyes, but he male has genes for both white and red eyes. (The fact that the male actually had red eyes tells us that red is dominant over white.) If the offspring get white from the female and white from the male, they will have white eyes. If they get white and red, they will have red eyes. The white eye gene is also linked to the chromosome that decides whether or not the insect will be male or female (shown here as a Y). It was by studying linkages such as this that Morgan was able to determine where the fruit fly's genes were located.

Horticultural Society in London on Mendel's work.

Thus, around 1900, three scientists arrived independently at the laws of inheritance, and reached a level of understanding where they recognized the full importance of Mendel's work. This understanding was due to developments in cell theory. Apart from Darwin's theory of natural selection, the most spectacular advances in biological studies in the second part of the nineteenth century was in the understanding of the structure and behavior of cells.

A Better Understanding of Cells

Nägeli had observed that some cells were formed by the division of other cells, but he thought that new cells could be formed out of the nucleus alone and believed that both cells and their nuclei could be formed in more than one way.

In 1856, pathologist Rudolf Virchow (1821–1902) published the results of his microscope work and rejected the idea that cells, or anything else, could arise by spontaneous generation. He argued that all cells were made out of already existing cells, *omnis cellula e cellula*, although he did not know how. Between 1852 and 1862, Robert Remak (1815–65) showed that cells divided by simple

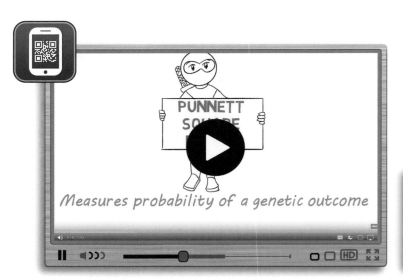

For a short video on Punnett squares, scan here:

constriction and that all the parts of the cell, the small dark-staining nucleus and the surrounding **cytoplasm**, were divided up at each cell division so that not only were all cells formed from pre-existing cells, but also nuclei appeared to be formed from pre-existing nuclei.

In 1861, French zoologist Eduard-Girard Balbiani (1825–99) had the idea of using a weak stain so that only parts of the cell stained. Until then, heavy stains had been used to color the entire object to be viewed under a microscope. Balbiani used a weak solution of carmine dye after fixing in acetic acid.

Balbiani's published pictures of preparations of conjugating single-cell ciliate animals show several stages of nuclear division: small darkly staining blobs arranged on a fibrous spindle. Balbiani thought these blobs were the spermatozoa of single-celled freshwater animals called "paramecium."

Theodor Schwann (1810–82) co-founder, with Schleiden, of the cell theory, had supposed in 1839 that an unfertilized egg could be considered a single cell with nucleus and cytoplasm and, in 1841, Albert Kölliker (1817–1905) had considered the spermatozoon to be a single nucleus. Then followed the observations of Amici in 1847 and of Pringsheim in 1856, who showed that single cells fuse at fertilization to provide the cell from which the new organism develops.

But it was not until 1876 that it was realized by Oscar Hertwig (1849–1922) that it is the nuclei that are important in fertilization. He saw two nuclei in a fertilized sea urchin egg and he realized that one of the nuclei was from the spermatozoon and the other from the egg cell. No one at this time, however, understood what happened to the nucleus in ordinary cell division and the generally held view was that the nucleus was dissolved away and then reformed in the two new cells after the cell had divided.

Fifteen years after his original publication, in which nuclear division was clearly figured though not recognized, Balbiani solved the problem.

In 1876, he at last understood the meaning of the dark staining blobs he had seen in paramecium. Working on the cells around the ovary of the grasshopper *Stenobothrus*, Balbiani saw that from the nucleus a number of blobs were formed. These batonnets, as he called them, became arranged in a bundle in the center

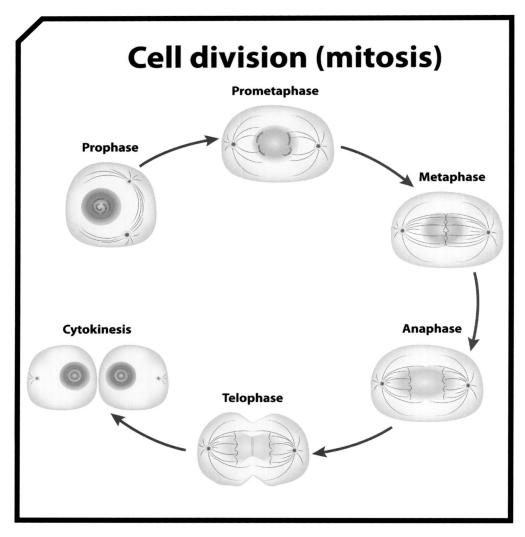

Cell division (mitosis)

Prometaphase

Prophase

Metaphase

Cytokinesis

Telophase

Anaphase

Today, we have a much better understanding of how genetic characteristics are carried in the cells. There are six stages in cell division, or mitosis. Just before a cell divides, the chromosomes, which carry genetic information, appear from the nucleus and double in number (prophase). Each pair then lines up along the middle of the cell (prometaphase). Next the members of each pair are pulled toward opposite end of the cell (metaphase). The sister chromatids move to opposite poles of the cell (anaphase), and a new nucleus is formed in each of the new cells (telophase). Finally the cell divides (cytokinesis). Both the new cells will have exactly the same number of chromosomes as there were in the original cell.

of the cell, divided in the middle and became two bundles, one of which went into each of the two new cells and formed the new nuclei.

This was the first record of the bodies now known as **chromosomes**, or "color bodies." They were given this name, in 1888, because they stained more heavily than the rest of the nucleus during cell division.

Balbiani was wrong in only one point. He said the batonnets divided in half across the middle whereas, in 1879, Walter Flemming (1843–1915) was able to show in salamander cells that the threads divided along their length. It was then quickly realized that this division of the nucleus by mitosis (Flemming's term, meaning "thread production") occurred in both plants and animals, from the single-cell protozoon to the higher organism.

Based on this recognition of chromosomes dividing equally at cell division, it was soon found that the chromosomes behaved differently during the formation of the eggs and spermatozoa, the egg cells and the pollen grains. Several cytologists (cell-biologists) contributed to the understanding that the number of chromosomes is reduced to half before the eggs and spermatozoa are ready for fertilization. Thus, the number typical of the organism is halved before fertilization and the typical number is again formed in the fertilized **zygote** from which the new organism grows by a long series of mitotic cell divisions.

In 1905, the division which halved the number of chromosomes in the germ cells became known as **meiosis** (reduction).

The advances were made as a result of improving techniques. Different stains were brought in to generate more selective pictures than Balbiani had obtained. Sometimes several stains were used to color different parts of the cell. The advances were made as each man recognized more than the one before. But a man sees only what he is looking for.

Balbiani had made preparations of chromosomes in the dividing nucleus of paramecium. But, because he thought the big nucleus of the protozoon was the ovary and the small one the testis, he saw spermatozoa instead of chromosomes. Many intermediate observations had to be made before Balbiani saw and understood the batonnets.

Understanding Heredity

One of the most important figures in the development of biological theory at this time was August Weismann (1834–1914), professor of zoology at the University of Freiburg in Germany. He was able to combine the ideas of inheritance with those of cytologists. Weismann showed that it is the **gametes** that are important in heredity.

Gametes (germ cells) fuse to form a cell from which a new organism is produced. Early in development, new gamete cells are made by this organism for sending on to the next generation. But the body cells of the organism die.

Weismann seems to have gained this idea from studying the growth of flies from eggs. He noticed that, early in development, cells were put aside that would eventually become the cells from which the gametes were made. From this, Weismann concluded that the body cells of the organism do not affect the hereditary capacities of the germ cells.

This made the inheritance of characteristics acquired during the life of an individual unlikely: cut off the tails of dogs or horses, generation after generation, but they still grow tails.

This was in agreement with what Mendel had found when he grew his different varieties of celandine side by side. They did not become like one another, but kept the inherited form of their ancestors. It argued against Darwin's idea of pangenes or **gemmules** that came from all over the body into the gametes and, in the next generation, determined the form of the organ from which they had come. Pangenes came from the whiskers, for example, to the gametes, were passed on at fertilization and determined and went into the cells of the whiskers of the new organism.

It was in the year of the batonnets, ten years after Mendel's paper, that de Vries started work on the hybridization of maize.

In 1889, de Vries published a book called *Intracellular Pangenesis*. His pangene was considered to be a definite material particle and all living organisms were made up of pangenes. De Vries believed that pangenes could be mixed together in any proportions and could explain the results of experiments in hybridization.

The seemingly endless variation in the form of the offspring of hybrids could be accounted for by the mixing of the pangenes in various ways.

Three years later, de Vries was investigating crosses between hairy and smooth white campions Silene. In the F^2 generation, he records the production of 392 hairy plants and 144 smooth. But de Vries deduced nothing from it.

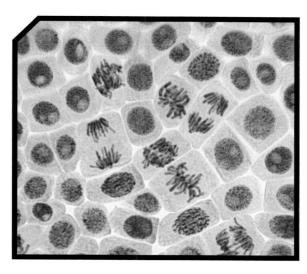

Chromosomes can only be seen when a cell is about to divide.

He crossed poppies with black marks at the base of the petals with a variety that has white marks at the base. In the second hybrid generation, he had 158 with black marks and 43 with white. The experiments were continued through several generations.

By 1896, de Vries knew about dominance and had discovered the 3 to 1 ratio of the F^2 generation. He also knew that of the three "dominant" types in the F^2 generation, only a third bred true and the other two-thirds were, like their parents, hybrid or **heterozygous** (Bateson's term in 1902 for combined unlike characteristics). De Vries planned his experiments to show how his pangenes, material particles, were inherited and how he had come to the same conclusions as Mendel. But he did not publish.

In 1899, when he gave an address to the International Conference of the Royal Horticultural Society, he did not reveal his results. He needed to prove that his theory held true for a great number of plants.

By the end of 1899, de Vries had evidence of the particulate nature of inheritance and segregation from over thirty different species and varieties. He was ready to publish.

Correns understood dominance and the 3 to 1 ratio, and that inherited factors could be considered to exist in pairs. He went further and suggested that the pairs of factors segregate sometime during the nuclear divisions that take place in the formation of the pollen grain and egg cell. Correns had the advantage over Mendel of the new cytology with its understanding of cell division.

Tschermak found that tall pea plants seemed to be dominant to short and he obtained a 3 to 1 ratio for yellow and green peas and for smooth and wrinkled.

The Mendelian laws had taken thirty-four years to be discovered by de Vries, Correns, and Tschermak. And it was only at this late date that their universality was recognized. None of the three had investigated or formalized the inheritance of more than one characteristic difference at the same time. Mendel's Law of Independent Assortment remained unique.

There was only one more piece to be put into the puzzle before the basic ideas of unit factor inheritance were complete.

In 1902, Correns related the inherited factors to the chromosomes. He supposed the factors to be like beads on a string, but he imagined that both factors of a pair were on the same chromosome. Finally, also in 1902, Walter Sutton (1877–1916) of Columbia University in the United States explained the relationship of Mendel's characteristics, or factors, to the chromosomes.

Working on grasshopper cells, Sutton showed that chromosomes occur in pairs: there are always two that look alike and that are usually distinguishable from all the others. *Brachystola magna*, the grasshopper, has twenty-two chromosomes—eleven pairs of chromosomes. Sutton suggested that this observation might "constitute the physical basis of the Mendelian law of heredity." Pairs of factors were carried on pairs of chromosomes.

Sutton then showed that the pairs of chromosomes come together and then separate, one into each gamete, during the reduction division of meiosis. This was the physical basis of segregation. So long as the characteristics were on different chromosomes, they would be inherited according to Mendel's Law of Independent Assortment.

This law could not always be true because the characteristics of an individual "could not exceed the number of chromosomes in the germ products," but as Sutton observed, "it follows that all the allelomorphs [factors] represented by any one chromosome must be inherited together."

Sutton established that many factors could be on the same chromosome and would be inherited together.

In 1909, Danish researcher Wilhelm Johannsen (1857–1927) gave the name *gene* to Mendel's factors.

If Mendel had never lived and worked in the monastery garden of Brno, the laws of heredity would have been discovered. The de Vriesian laws, as they would have been called, would have made the same impact. The time was right, in 1900, for the laws of heredity to be understood.

 ## TEXT-DEPENDENT QUESTIONS

1. How long did Mendel continue his experiments with Hieracium?
2. What disease did Mendel die of in 1884?
3. What author referred to Mendel's work in his 1869 book on species and varieties?
4. Who sent a copy of Mendel's 1865 paper to Hugo de Vries?

 ## RESEARCH PROJECT

Using the internet or your school library, find out more about one of the three scientists who independently confirmed Mendel's research around 1900: Hugo de Vries, Erich von Tschermak, or Carl Correns. Write a two-page report about this scientists's life and contributions to the field of genetics, and share it with your class.

Chronology

1753
Linnaeus records two hybrid plants as new species.

1760
Kölreuter makes first experimental plant hybrids.

1822
Johann Mendel born in July.

1833
Mendel goes to school in Lipnik.

1834
Transfers to the Imperial Royal Gymnasium in Opava.

1841
Studies at the Philosophical Institute at Olomouc.

1843
Admitted to the Augustinian Monastery in Brno and takes the name of Gregor.

1847
Mendel is ordained.

1849
Appointed supply teacher at the Imperial Royal High School of Znojmo.

1850
Fails his teachers' qualifying examination.

1851
Goes to Vienna University to study physics and biology.

Mendel studied the characteristics of bee colonies at the monastery, but never published the results of his research.

1853
Mendel reads paper to the Zoological and Botanical Society of Vienna on a moth pest of radishes. Appointed supply teacher in physics and natural history at the Brno Technical School.

1854
A letter from Mendel on the pea weevil read to the Zoological and Botanical Society of Vienna.

1856
Mendel starts experiments on *Pisum*.

1859

On the Origin of Species by Means of Natural Selection by Charles Darwin is published.

1863

Mendel's experiments on *Pisum* completed.

1865

In February and March, Mendel reads his paper *Experiments in Plant Hybridization* to the Brno Natural History Society.

1866

Experiments in Plant Hybridization by Mendel is published.

1868

Mendel elected abbot of the monastery.

1884

Mendel dies on January 6 in Brno.

1900

Carl Correns publishes a paper, "G. Mendel's Law of the Behavior of the Progeny of Hybrid Races," based on his own versions of Mendel's experiments. He and other scientists, including Erich Tschermak von Seysenegg, Hugo de Vries, and William Jasper Spillman, bring Mendel's discoveries into the mainstream and develop the field of genetics.

Further Reading

Bortz, Fred. *The Laws of Genetics and Gregor Mendel*. New York: Rosen, 2014.

Edelson, Edward. *Gregor Mendel and the Roots of Genetics*. New York: Oxford University Press, 1999.

Henig, Robin Marantz. *The Monk in the Garden: The Lost and Found Genius of Gregor Mendel, the Father of Genetics*. New York: Houghton Mifflin Company, 2001.

Lieberman, Philip. *The Theory that Changed Everything: "On the Origin of Species" as a Work in Progress*. New York: Columbia University Press, 2018.

Mendel, Gregor. *Experiments in Plant Hybridisation*. Trans. by William Bateson. (1865). New York: Pantianos Classics, 2017.

Morus, Iwan Rhys. *The Oxford Illustrated History of Science*. New York: Oxford University Press, 2017.

Pierce, Benjamin A. *Genetics: A Conceptual Approach*. New York: W. H. Freeman and Company, 2014.

Wootton, David. *The Invention of Science: A New History of the Scientific Revolution*. New York: Harper Perennial, 2016.

Internet Resources

http://ghr.nlm.nih.gov/handbook/basics/dna

Information on genetics and DNA is provided by the National
Institutes of Health.

https://www.genome.gov/26524120

The National Human Genome Research Institute provides facts and
information about chromosomes at this website.

www.darwins-theory-of-evolution.com

This website provide an overview of Darwin's theory of evolution, with
links to articles and videos that help to explain the theory.

www.sciencenewsforstudents.org

Science News for Students is an award-winning online publication
dedicated to providing age-appropriate, topical science news to
learners, parents and educators.

www.pbs.org/wgbh/nova

The website of NOVA, a science series that airs on PBS. The series
produces in-depth science programming on a variety of topics, from the
latest breakthroughs in technology to the deepest mysteries of the natural
world.

http://evolution.berkeley.edu/evolibrary/article/evo_01

This website, sponsored by the University of California at Berkeley,
provides an introduction to evolution and the origins of life.

Series Glossary of Key Terms

anomaly—something that differs from the expectations generated by an established scientific idea. Anomalous observations may inspire scientists to reconsider, modify, or come up with alternatives to an accepted theory or hypothesis.

evidence—test results and/or observations that may either help support or help refute a scientific idea. In general, raw data are considered evidence only once they have been interpreted in a way that reflects on the accuracy of a scientific idea.

experiment—a scientific test that involves manipulating some factor or factors in a system in order to see how those changes affect the outcome or behavior of the system.

hypothesis—a proposed explanation for a fairly narrow set of phenomena, usually based on prior experience, scientific background knowledge, preliminary observations, and logic.

natural world—all the components of the physical universe, as well as the natural forces at work on those things.

objective—to consider and represent facts without being influenced by biases, opinions, or emotions. Scientists strive to be objective, not subjective, in their reasoning about scientific issues.

observe—to note, record, or attend to a result, occurrence, or phenomenon.

science—knowledge of the natural world, as well as the process through which that knowledge is built through testing ideas with evidence gathered from the natural world.

subjective—referring to something that is influenced by biases, opinions, and/or emotions. Scientists strive to be objective, not subjective, in their reasoning about scientific issues.

test—an observation or experiment that could provide evidence regarding the accuracy of a scientific idea. Testing involves figuring out what one would expect to observe if an idea were correct and comparing that expectation to what one actually observes.

theory—a broad, natural explanation for a wide range of phenomena in science. Theories are concise, coherent, systematic, predictive, and broadly applicable, often integrating and generalizing many hypotheses. Theories accepted by the scientific community are generally strongly supported by many different lines of evidence. However, theories may be modified or overturned as new evidence is discovered.

Index

About the Author

George Wilmer lives in Poughkeepsie, New York, with his wife Cindy and their children Irene and Nicholas. A graduate of the State University of New York at Stony Brook, he works in the pharmaceutical industry. This is his first book.

Photo Credits

used under license from Shutterstock, Inc.: 6, 8, 11, 12, 13, 14, 18, 22, 28, 30, 37, 38, 44, 47, 50, 53, 55, 57, 59, 66, 69, 80, 83; vvoe / shutterstock.com: 32; Thomas Hunt Morgan (*A Critique of the Theory of Evolution* [1916], p. 74): 77; U.S. National Library of Medicine: 1, 74, 75; Wellcome Library: 15, 17, 34, 36, 40, 52, 68, 72; Wikimedia Commons: 10, 25, 29, 43, 63.